Winnie-the-Pooh's

Learning Fun

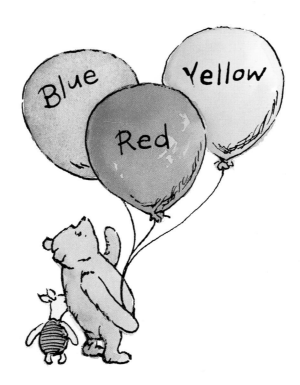

Inspired by A. A. MILNE
With Decorations by ERNEST H. SHEPARD

DUTTON CHILDREN'S BOOKS

Published by Dutton Children's Books, a division of Penguin Putnam Inc.,
345 Hudson Street, New York, NY 10014

Printed in Hong Kong

ISBN 0-525-46322-4

Inspired by
A. A. Milne

Winnie-the-Pooh's
ABC

with illustrations by
Ernest H. Shepard

Dutton Children's Books
New York

Published in the United States by Dutton Children's Books,
a division of Penguin USA
375 Hudson Street
New York, New York 10014

Designed by Joseph Rutt

Printed in Hong Kong
First Edition
ISBN 0-525-45365-2
10 9 8 7

A a

apple

B b

balloon

C c

cow

D d

dragon

E e

Eeyore

F f

forest

G g

gate

H h

honey

I i

island

J j

jump

K k

Kanga

L l

lion

M m

mirror

N n

North Pole

O o

Owl

P p

Piglet

Q q

queen

R r

Rabbit

S s

T t

U u

umbrella

V v

violets

W w

Winnie-the-Pooh

X x

expotition

Y y

yellow daffodils

Z z

zoo

Inspired by
A. A. Milne

Winnie-the-Pooh's
Colors

With Decorations by
Ernest H. Shepard

Dutton Children's Books
NEW YORK

Published in the United States by
Dutton Children's Books,
a division of Penguin Books USA Inc.
375 Hudson Street
New York, New York 10014

Designed by Joseph Rutt
Printed in Hong Kong
First Edition
ISBN 0-525-45428-4
7 9 10 8

Pooh's sweater
is red.

Piglet wears a
red scarf.

Christopher Robin's front door is green.

Piglet wears a
green sweater.

Pooh floats under
a blue balloon.

The sky is blue.

Christopher Robin
wears a yellow hat.

The bee is black
and yellow.

Piglet picks purple flowers.

Pooh has a purple
honey pot.

Tigger is orange.

Pooh and Piglet
walk toward an
orange sunset.

Rabbit is brown.

Eeyore's house is made of brown sticks.

Pooh is gold.

Pooh's honey
is gold.

Eeyore is gray.

The heffalump
is gray.

Pooh sits in a pink chair.

The bathtub is pink.

Snow is white.

Christopher Robin
wears a white shirt.

The umbrella
is black.

Christopher Robin's boots are black.

Inspired by A. A. MILNE

Winnie-the-Pooh's
1·2·3

With illustrations by

ERNEST H. SHEPARD

Dutton Children's Books

NEW YORK

Published in the United States by Dutton Children's Books,
a division of Penguin Books USA Inc.
375 Hudson Street, New York, New York 10014
Printed in Hong Kong
First Edition
ISBN 0-525-45534-5
3 5 7 9 10 8 6 4 2

one balloon

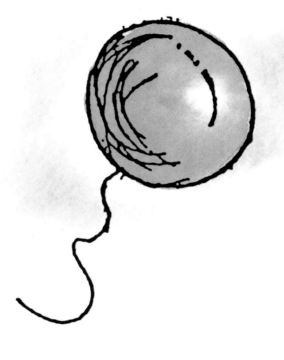

two umbrellas

three bells

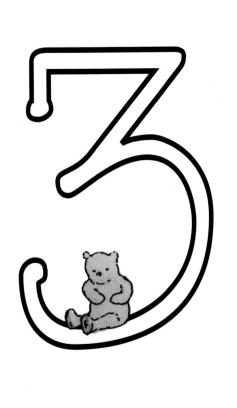

four candles

five beetles

six boots

seven baskets

eight birds

nine dandelions

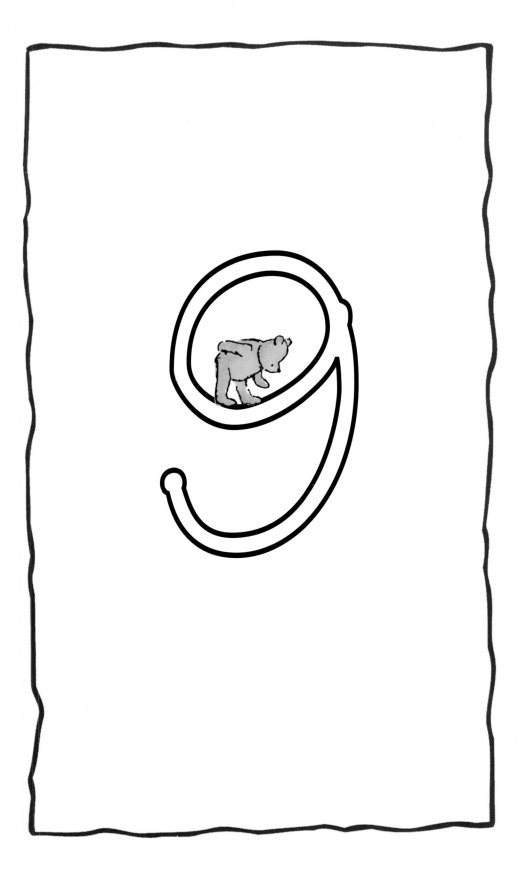

ten honey pots

eleven trees

twelve bees

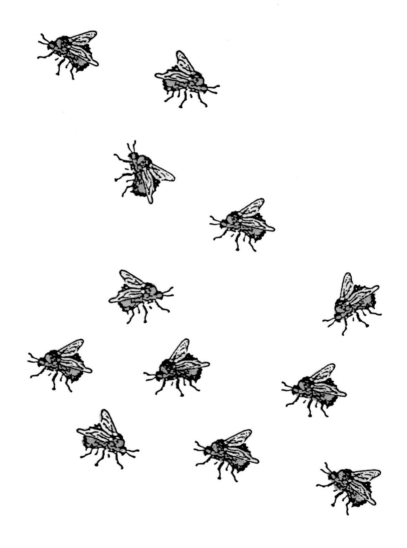

Inspired by
A. A. Milne

Winnie-the-Pooh's
Opposites

With Decorations by
Ernest H. Shepard

Dutton Children's Books
New York

Published in the United States by
Dutton Children's Books,
a division of Penguin Books USA Inc.
375 Hudson Street
New York, New York 10014

Designed by Joseph Rutt
Printed in Hong Kong
First Edition
ISBN 0-525-45429-2
5 7 9 10 8 6

up

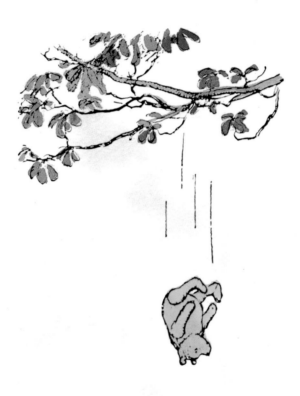

down

in

out

happy

sad

dirty

clean

awake

asleep

front

back

top

bottom

loud

quiet

wet

dry

on

warm

cold

large

small

Inspired by A. A. MILNE

Winnie-the-Pooh Tells Time

With Decorations by

ERNEST H. SHEPARD

Dutton Children's Books

NEW YORK

7:00 a.m.

It's seven o'clock.

Good morning, Pooh.

8:00 a.m.

It's **eight** o'clock.

Time for breakfast.

10:00 a.m.

It's **ten** o'clock.

Pooh does his
exercises.

11:00 a.m.

It's **eleven** o'clock.

Time for a little
smackerel of
something.

12:00 p.m.

It's **twelve** o'clock.

Lunchtime.

1:00 p.m.

It's **one** o'clock.

Pooh sings a
new song.

2:00 p.m.

It's **two** o'clock.

Pooh wants
another smackerel.

3:00 p.m.

It's **three** o'clock.

Pooh

practices

jumping.

4:00 p.m.

It's **four** o'clock.

Pooh and Piglet go
to Owl's house for
a Proper Tea.

5:00 p.m.

It's **five** o'clock.

Time for a game of
Poohsticks.

6:00 p.m.

It's **six** o'clock.

Dinnertime.

8:00 p.m.

It's **eight** o'clock.

Good night, Pooh.